DUMPSTERFIRE PRESS
(GRAND RAPIDS, MI)
USA

Art by Dillinger

Cover design by Dillinger

Edited by Mike Zone

ISBN: 9798809188227

Manufactured in the United States of America.

Milenko Županovic's work can be a lot to take in with an unflinching view of the world derived from esoteric mystical texts of both an Old Testament tone yet a New Testament blessing of peace offered after all the flames have been burned out and the blood washed away.

Dillinger and I have the had the honor of publishing two of his previous works; **IMMORTAL DREAMS** and **PSALM OF LAST DAYS** which has had some people questioning of why we were publishing this type of work in the first place…doesn't it stand for everything **DFP** against?

When we started this press, it was give voices to those seldom heard…this isn't necessarily dogma or a theological treatise as it is a journey throughout an ancient world reconciling itself with a world on fire descending somewhere we can never be sure where…

The volume you hold in your hands offers a perspective with a bit of history, theology, and philosophy. You'll find poetry and prose from both the two previous volumes with new material completing a trilogy that takes us out of the world of dreams through the last days into visions of what may come to be in order to find a salvation of sorts.

While reading this won't result in immortality it may plant new seeds of contemplation to grapple with a herculean set of revelations about to crash down upon our ever-fluctuating mortal realm teetering between rigid order of a satiric nature or wild insanity.

Mike Zone

Golgotha

In cold

chambers

death

gruesome shadows

sinners

disappear

in the dark

depths

faith

on the hill

of crucifixion.

Blood of Apostle

On the night

a divided

heaven

light

of the Gods

disappears

in darkness

of time.

Votive tiles

Every night in the desolate cathedral,

he would awaken him with an unknown sound,

like a heartbeat.

There were thousands of silver tile in the sea,

in the middle of it there was something like the sun,

but he could not see what it was.

Nobody for centuries find these tiles,

because there is a story that

they are silver gifts to a church,

far from that place.

Unbelievers robbed this sacred place

and put the silver in with it.

After a few days they are dead into the storm

and the plates spilled over to the surface

and since then no one is touching them.

The architect thinks that he only sent it to heaven

and that he was better protected

and taken to a sacred place, so he decided to decorate his
cathedral.

In the middle, the light was shrinking each day,

a tile in the shape of the golden heart

of the Sagrada Familia was adorned with silver plates,

the heart is bleeding.

Faith of the sea

In the depths of the soul

the vision of the world,

 God and man,

saints and apostles,

 people and temptations

one night he dreamed

of a painter trapped

 in the depths of the sea,

Every night he dreamed

of another painter,

 sitting at the bottom

 of the sea

with his blood painted

 in the heavenly gallery

of that chapel

the ingredients of eternity,

 sea salt and his own blood.

The last apostle

The entire wall

was covered

with it

night was mystical

as the picture

that ended

Monastery

of Santa Maria

was decorated

as the most beautiful

flower

The apostles

in the picture

Judas is behind them

The artist finished

his work,

and went to eternity

the lightning flashes

revealed a mystical work

they could only see

the blood flowing

in the place where

the reflection it was

as the presence

of another apostle

Leonardo beside

the apostles

blood on the walls

of the monastery.

RIO NEGRO

They thought
 that for him
 there is no more
 salvation
 and decided on the last,
 desperate move
Early in the dawn,
 they went by boat
 to the outer limits coast
pushed the black river
 and sailed away.
With arms crossed
over his chest
some invisible force
blue eyes in the darkness
 of the forest
 that surrounded the river,
 and then appeared for a while
when he heard
 that all whispering '
Rio Negro, Rio Negro,
was dropped into the black river
the blackness disappeared,
and then he saw
a beautiful blue color
 as if it was not of this world.
When he turned, he saw
 birds that passed by him,
far in the air
nobody can dream
He then began to descend rapidly
" Lord, hear my prayer "
he said quietly
" Rio Negro, and receive my prayer

echoed in the distance.

Dark stars

Soul hides

 a secret

 priest at

confession

final departure

heaven for

forgiveness

to the final

destination

 the light

 disappears

 in the open sky

 with dark star

in his embrace

Reflection

Unreal
pictures

heavenly

life

reflections

of death

in the mirror

of eternity.

Magdalene

Salvation

from goblins

under cross

at Calvary

open

grave

grace

of God

hidden

messages

to whisper

Apostles.

Way of the Cross

Forgiveness

of sins

confession

front

of the image
Lord
refuge
prayers
final
sunset

Shaman

The road through the jungle

 was very difficult

discover the mystical religion

 in the heart of Brazil

light we saw the other day,

In the distance

 we could hear the sounds

of drums echoed

 through the forest

Skeleton danced

and formed a circle

in the corner stood a man

and in his eyes there was despair

He wanted to escape

from that place

only when the music mute,

he could see the real picture

rhythm of drums

echoed through the woods

Everyone danced as delirious,

green light is covered all,

Amazon had a heart

that was beating

the rhythm of the music

and the lyrics

that are repeated

" Daima Force daime amor ".

BLACK ANCHORS

Legend

about the ship

with slaves from

an unknown place

that took shelter

big storm

symbols mystical

magical powers

the sound of

heavy chain

hitting the ground

causing fear among

the population

unknown force

pulling the chains

bound edges at sea

as ghosts

shadows in the night

to the sea

black statues at sea

unknown symbols

island with black anchors

still standing.

Bones

Ghosts

of missing

Apostle

of faith

an open

grave

of prophets

times.

Angel

The stars
of night
in the eyes
of lost
angel
to shoulder

the wind
of unbelief

Atlantis

Lament on the land

pinch the flower

from the book of civilization

I cry every time

When I see dry land

bandaged in black

suffering for homeland

I cry and pray

last trace of beauty

hidden within us.

Resurrection

In the dark
of missing memories
the soul
of righteous
shadow of the Cross
covers
ash
defunct
flame
faith.

Immortality

Tears of blood

in the shadow

 of the Cross
on the hill

 of crucifixion
extinguished

 candles
of missing heaven.

Solar Eclipse

Shadow of Moon

is fell asleep

on the Earth

as darkness

covers fear

in my dreams

sinful.

Crystal Skull

It has long dreamed

 about them,

read all the books

mystical work of

ancient peoples

Latin America,

object from the ground

 a perfect work

 of human hands

 Archaeologist

 removed

 the remains

 of his works

buried deep

in the woods,

skull stared at him

a prisoner

to their pyramid

human heads

were rolling down

a machete was flashed

to his head

died in the arms

of a skeleton

The crystal skull

 is looking towards

the surface of the lake

The lake was red,

 the color of the blood

 of the martyrs

of the sacred pyramids.

Prayer

Dark star
in the heart of graves
prayer spirits
on the ashes

of centuries
black ground
covered.

FIELDS

The King stood proudly

 in his black uniform

Hunters had weapons

ready on black horses

On the end were placed

cannon, the last link

of that chain

In front of them

stands the infantry,

 ready to die for his King

Queen looking at him

The war last for centuries,

 the battle does't solve anything

The battlefield was transformed

 into black and white

For centuries, the fields were left

 soaked in their colors,

and now we stand on them

This field will again paint our colors

Of blood and death.

Apocalypse

In a deserted church
call for help
take off the dust
the walls
watch fresco
shivering
fear.

Stone Graves

Cult of the Dead
unclear symbols
carved in stone
sank into the ground
eternal sleepers
forgotten secrets.

Isaac

Tears
in the eye
of a blind
prophet
mirror
of victims
commands
of God.

Pain

Burned
verses
of a missing
love
pain
of a defunct
heart
covered
by ash.

Mount

Lost
Worlds
of bloody sky
resurrection
of prayers
on the hill
where eternal
dark watches.

Ashes
The sin
burned
at the stake of faith
ashes of truth
covering traces of
lost mortals.

Sadness

Broken wings
cold nights
morning of hope
sadness in the eyes
of the lost angel.

Psalms

Screams
from the abyss
spiritual
desolation
prayer
in the clouds
tears
hidden.

Flash

Cold views
disappearing in the fog
looking
for mythical
kiss of death.

Gaudi

Architect of dreams
the battle is lost
surreal cathedral
the grave is brought

Forgiveness

Bloody thorns
rain has washed
while on the ground
is intact
waiting for God
to take it
in His arms
and forgive
those
who had it spilled.

Coat of Arms

Gold letters
of a past
hidden for centuries
remain engraved
in the crown
blazon of prefect
sitting
on the throne
of eternity.

Tears

Heaven's shadow
hid their
eyes
full of tears
melted hope
on the candle flame
a last prayer.

Ikon Lamp

Melted candles
in the arms of silver
light penetrates
through sinkhole
the human soul
shadow of the rosette
the flame of faith.

Spark

Passing river
under the bridge
applies flame
from the ashes of youth
wrinkled face in the water
reflect the old man
hiding the tears
the last spark.

Birth

A spark of faith
mother's body
the secret of the universe
God smiles
in the eyes of a child.

Land of Hope

Desperate in the dark
wounded and lost
seeks salvation
look in the sky
fifty-two stars
illuminate my path
I look at the statue
with the flame of freedom.

Pictures

Fear
never before

as far
cold pictures
from an unknown
in the lives of
long dead.

Ocean

In the eyes

of dead sea

 screams

of crew

ship

at the bottom

ocean.

Sinners

Blue

icons

heaven

in heart

of sinner

prayers

in judgement

day.

Blue

The blood of poets

Glorious

past

ancestors

in the veins

verses

blood

poets

in the sky

discovered.

Glory

Abandoned

heart

in the labyrinth

of nothing

death

in the dark

of light.

Crying

Bloody

tears

down

 the face

of Virgin

 disappeared

sins

of crying

prayers.

Dreams of the Gods

Prayer

of silence

whisper

of gods

in dreams

immortal.

Skull

Bloody tears

in the night

down the face

of hill

in the form

of skull

in place

of where

eternal

 darkness

shines.

Youth

Prayer
on the coast
Bay of
dreams
lost
source
of youth.

RASPUTIN

Loved by the Empress

He talked to the Virgin

Killed several times

Walk the valley blind

A broken heart

Without hope of coming back

Become dust and ashes.

CORPUS CHRISTI

Ostensorium
in a procession

of almost

the entire city,

it leads to

the statue

of the saint

on the hill,

relics returned

to the church

a stranger,

only in a white

slept next to

the statue

of the saint

thorns stuck

into his hand,

blood trickled

down by snow

boards of the city,

he cried

and so fell asleep

everybody was crying,
strangers were buried
next to the statue
crying that echoed
the empty church.
Jesus the Savior.

Stone soldiers

The place of the nameless

through the gates

into the memory

of the space

a man with dreams

about the past

the fear of the people

of the unknown

the dreams of his work.

the bloody dreams of a place

without names,

looks back to the memories

of the architects of the past

in the eyes of a man

who is no longer there

the bridge that only exists

in his dreams

the river of books

eleven soldiers hold the stones

on their backs,

the writer of the creature,

their birth, eternal life,

the guard of the ages,

the heart of the creator

in the eye of the bridge.

The seventh day

The protection

of the helpless

the witness

of the desperate

hope of the innocent

the seventh day

creation of life

on the bright side

of the death.

Storm
Tears
of heaven
guardians
eternal
dreams
in arms
of dark
clouds.

Darkness

Reflection
of eternity
in the mirror
where
eternal

darkness

shines.

Resurrection

In the dark
of missing memories
the soul
of righteous
shadow of the Cross
covers
ash
defunct
flame
faith.

Island of the Dead

Pictures
of future
in the mind
of prophet
deserted
island
dead
mouth
speak.

Meditation

Mystical

                              vision

    of space

                              creation

of new

             world

                              dreams

hidden.

Black Flags

to embrace
  light
  like a shadow
  month
  on earth
  trapped.

Life

Solitude
cold
views
a vanished sparks
of hope time
past life.

Time

Verses
disperse
on the sky
return to poetry
in time of penance

Ground

Blood traces
of sins
without remorse
ground covering

Echoes

The sound
dark depths
echoes
passage
lost
time

Light

In the heart of remorse
grace
a hermit
brings
light
pure forgiveness.

Dust

Spirit

of apostles
            the gallows
            figure of betrayal
                        in silver
    dust

    disappears.

**Apparitions
death
disappear
in a fog
recollections
verses
dead
poet
hidden.**

Desperation

*Spiritual
desolation
dark
heart
hidden
in the
ground.*

Dreams of centuries

Burned bridges

of freedom
dead silence
in the abyss
of death
gruesome shadows
salvation army
dreams of centuries
in prison of infinity.

Fates
Magic
East
light
tombs
burned
bridges
death
fate
abandoned
gates
heaven
disappear
in the fog.

JuDaS

Spirit

  of apostles

          the gallows
          figure of betrayal
          in silver

       dust

disappears.

Secret

Extinct
eyes
light
faith
reveals
secret
new
life
with black
earth
covered.

My God

King wanted
to build a

hill in this place

works are going

very slowly

his insane ideas

workers have died

 in this place

when King was

already old,

ordered the

construction stops

the sun is shining

 on a rock

Along the valley

echoed my God, my God

At that moment,

everyone knelt

and began to cry,

except the king,

who all watched silently

It seemed

the sun is crying

He had something
to tell me,
to convey
a secret message
The sun is shining
on my face
 and I sank
 into eternity
My God, my God ....

the sun is crying

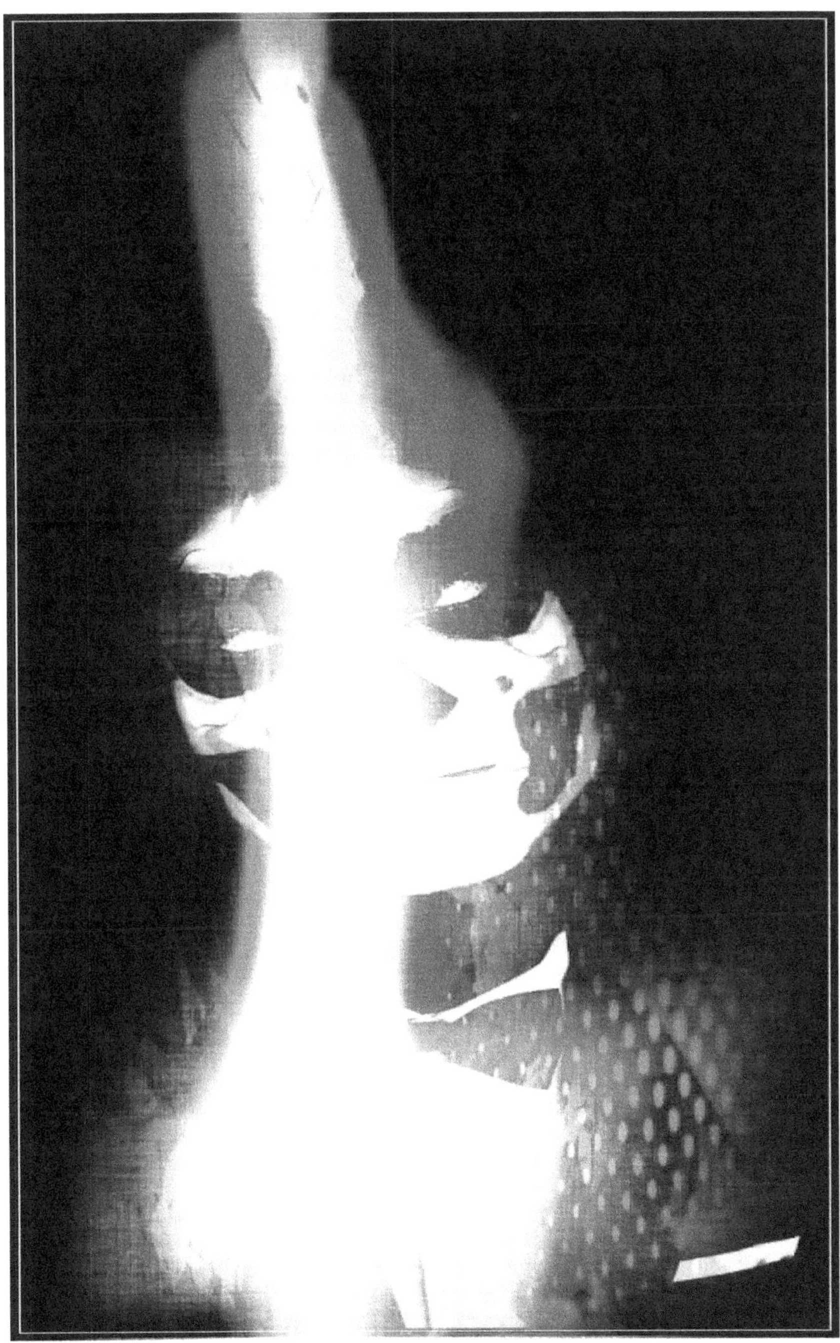

Requiem

Legend that lasts

confession of

unknown artist,

whisper in the garden

a requiem for

the healing

of the soul

flying towards

the clouds

for the last star

whisper a prayer

to the small town

over the sea

for eternity

legend that lasts

on a desert island

the silence of eternity

lighted candles

in church with

artist of sorrow.

Monastery of Silence

Priest every night

says a prayer

near the church

with the blue dome,

in a dream

music the last time

an unnamed grave

silence echoes

before sleep

strange visions

music dreams

enigma forever

at the door

garden full of flowers

through the light

of faith

the music of the past

through dreams

reaching out to him

with a cross

in his hands

a requiem for

forgiveness

an unknown grave,

dream prayers

light in centuries.

Mirror

Pictures

of last
life
    hidden
    in the dark
    of quarters
    consciousness.

surreal

                image

                in the secret

                chambers

                of the *universe*

                dark matter

                covered.

Eternally obscuration

Eyes looking
out of the darkness
light fight
with demons
who tearing
every emotion
tired eyes
spark disappears.

My hands are bloody
trying to overcome barriers
scratching on the rocks
I'm looking for the light
that does not have

 fear overtakes me
at the thought of
eternal abyss.

WITHOUT FACE

That night

I was back home

late

very tired

I was driving

like a maniac

lost control

a stranger came out

in front of me

and I hit him

started to

 run away

three of them

in black

without words

they put me

in their car

none of them

had a face

place of death

there was

a church build

When I went in

music they played

was loud

the people

turned to me ...

None of them

had a face

I saw the face

of a stranger

That was me ...

Oh Lord, help me

When I looked

in the mirror

I saw a man

without face.

STONE MOSES

Blood on his face, creator has unsuccessfully tried to stop the bleeding, but nothing.

His masterpiece, it was over, stone Moses was no longer in a position in which it was carved.

His hand pointed toward the frescos on the wall of the chapel, but no one knew what he had in mind, because of an endless series of characters on the wall it was difficult to single out one.

When his creator moved closer, to stone Moses changed his position and grabbed him by the neck, he is almost out of breath.

Michelangelo could not breathe, Moses with knife plunged into his chest.

The character of the frescoes was trying to free the artist, his face was pressed against his face.

Saint Barthelemy is still holding the bloody knife in his hand.

Then he quickly returned to the gallery of the figure on the wall, Michelangelo picked up his hummer, and Moses returned to the position in which it was carved, but he had a smile on his face.

The priest approached Michelangelo and something told him in confidence.

Saint Barthelemy watched them from the wall, when his blood felt down face .

Heavenly forces are holding him.

While returning to the chapel, he saw an object falling slowly on the floor .

Quickly he approached and saw that it was the skin of Saint Barthelemy.

On his skin he engraved the figure of Michelangelo.

Stone Moses was pointing toward the frescoes on the wall.

My goodness

The valley was sunny but j one place was in the shade, can not fit into the whole ambience.

For years it was so, ordinary people it is interpreted differently, but only the king was displeased, he thought it was a bad sign for his empire, because he issued a special order.

He wanted to build a hill in this place, and that's why the poor forced to carry stones per correct answer schedule, who would not or could not have been thrown into slavery.

The works are going very slowly, that's a bunch of stones was all the greater, as the sun retreated, has not wanted to make that touches the ground at that point.

Everything seemed to be the king decided to go in his insane ideas and up to the sky.

Over time, many workers have died in this place, of old age or exhaustion, and the valley echoed my God ...

From the pile of stones, a small stone separated from them, and went their separate ways.

After many years when King was already old, ordered the construction stops.

However, just then, the sun is shining on a pile of rocks, mountain shone, while all axis melts were the dark.

Along the valley echoed my God, my God ...

At that moment, everyone knelt and began to cry, except the king, who all watched silently.

Someone is going, he is difficult step, but no one was not allowed to help.

Small stone continued his journey, crossed a large part, even got into the ocean.

All were crying and their wages were increasing, when a man came to the top of the hill.

**Then the sun retreated again, from that place, and illuminated the valley, but the people knelt and wept.
In the valley ringing my God, my God ...
It seemed as if the sun is crying, grieving for him, a shade that covered the valley, was in the form of cross.
In the valley ringing " My God, my God, why leave me? "**

**Small stone has come a long way and came up to me.
He had something to tell me, to convey a secret message.
The sun is shining on my face and I sank into eternity.
My God, my God ....**

Flight

Traces

 wings

 held

 to the skin

 bloody

 wounds

 earthly

 fall.

In the shade
of lamps
speech

With

silence
in the Night
of creation.

Penance

Rhyme
spill
in the sky
firmament
return
poetry
at time
penance.

Solitude
cold
views
disappeared

in sparks
of hope

time
past life.

Kingdom

Whisper

of darkness
secrets
symbol
in prohibited
kingdom.

Judgment days

Collapsed
dreams
mortal
In desperation
judgment
days.

Saints

In the Egyptian desert, prayer in the air, the legend about the origin in an ancient tomb in golden letters written memories.

Hordes of demons in the year of the wilderness, the cry from the grave, the light in the sand, hordes are getting closer, changing shape, a saint in heaven hermit in prayer, the girl in the river.

River which cuts the desert in two parts, a girl with two faces, that's right, a saint in heaven, swarms of insects in the direction of the desert, the girl was washing with fresh water, the face of an old woman.

In the ruined tomb, insects from the sky, the desert turns into the lake, extreme cold, prayers to heaven Gazette on ice, the girl in the river, destroyed the tombs, are almost silent prayer, meditation, freedom, salvation from death messenger of joy, empty tomb, from the depths hearts fire saints, sign in heaven, the cross from the clouds.

Insects are on the ground, the girl with two faces lucky fish in the form of the gondola, the bells of the church of St. Marc, the sound of the harp cannot be canceled meditation saints painting on canvas of golden sand, sin without prayer, hallucinations in the desert, religion embossed gold seal.

The sin of unbelief in the form of a horde of hell girl with two faces regretted, leaving the gondola to the sound of bells, an oasis in the desert, St. Mark's Church to pray for the survivors, beggars and sinners.

Ancient tomb hides a secret, a painter with a vision, without redemption, the madness of the moment, the fire of saints, a hermit in prayer, unreal church in the distance. A voice from the heart tells him to persevere, for the girl from the river, prayers are heard, a voice from the grave was silent, the last move, master painting, surrounded by skulls in a windowless room, strewn with land in the heart of the fire of the saints for the new morning, a painter of sinners, thorns on the road, a hermit goes to the Lord, the prayers of the sky, surreal church in the distance sends kisses in the morning.

Anger

Voice of truth

comes to you

without anger
opens doors
of freedom.

Crib

A star has fallen

follow its trail

Take me to the crib

The kings have already come

I pray in silence

I know it's not the end.

Is not the end

Dive into darkness

Avoid octopus of

death

that blindly search you

touch the bottom

with a scar on the soul

emerge on the surface.

View

Constant search

for the remaining parts

of childhood

turned into a quest

for the rest of their lives

and sinks

looking at us

eyes closed.

River of salvation

Dark Forces

haunt me in my sleep

through the forest

going to find salvation

the forces captured my neck

trying to drown me

but I disappear into the depths of the river

which flows into the sea of poetry.

The survival of the faith

A smile of hope

in old photographs

blues with the rest of your life

for disabled

with tied hands

and chains on their feet.

Mysticism

The Mystical Body

hover above us

hug us

 pray for us

suffer the sins of us all

with a prayer on their lips.

Church on the island

Magic shines

out of the blue dome

which merges with the sky

captures my soul

Heaven gives

Church on the island

surrounded by sea.

Martyrs

The white cross in the sea

at holy site

rocks

stained with blood

churches on the coast

symbols of eternity

sign mortals.

DEVIL'S JUMP

He saw a man in red costume, he came to him, but a man was on the floor corded, he doesn't move.

A man in red costume became fat, he walk with obstacle, but he must do it his work, his obligation.

Than a man in red suit fell down on a man on the floor and flattened him.

Oh, again that nightmare, said a man.

Every night he doesn't not sleep, lonely in his house, but he does not escape a man with burning legs, and then he blast him.

Oh, again that nightmares, I must stop with this, said a man, lonely man.

On the ritual, with a suite of devil, every year he was a man who jump over a children.

This is sign that the ghoul walk away.

But in that moment, he fell down and flattened...this was an accident.

But every night he was awake, he does not sleep.

Than in the night a man in red suit took him , a put it in front of that city , corded.

Every man in the city was dressed in suite of devil.

They jump over him, but everyone slap down, and flattened him.

Then every nightmare came away.

The cope of heaven

Bright lamps

in the night

illuminates the dome

reflection makes

to be painted

saints

move on the sky

churches on the coast.

Icon of the Virgin

They remained alone on the shore, while the parents went to morning mass, a feast for the eyes, church flags, wind them slow moving, shout to God with the lips of the faithful, before an icon of her, for the benefit of all, in the chapel on the island, with the blue dome and shine votive tiles, before the open sky, looking at the magical view of mothers, children on the shore, awaiting the return of their parents, under the open sky, the three of them, play in the sand, rough sea, sailing in passing, to the rhythm of the waves, jump over bodies on the coast, sand move, the lamp is in the church on the island of shiny, before the open sky, the three boys, unbearable heat and desire for shade on the other side of the coast, in front of the closed sea and great depths, get a photo of God with love, before an icon of a shiny, on the altar of the ancestors, the Old Testament sibyls, rigid views of fathers, parents in the chapel, rough sea, the boys in it, one does not want to surrender before the challenge, prayer of the faithful in front of the open sky, the light penetrates into the depths of shiny, dark lady heart unfaithful, the challenge is all the greater, the two go by the coast , the smallest loses power, waves cover the body, with blue dome chapel, hall of reconciliation, cry beat, no one can hear in the church with the choir in the glory of God, hidden tears of mothers, boys on the coast, do not see the slightest, adrift, great depth, front morning mass, with a prayer on his lips, faith light in front of the open sky, the dark heart catching body and dragged it to the bottom, no one heard his cry, frightened eyes of boys, the end of the ceremony, with choirs singing to God, a cry of love, views towards the coast, there is no one, crying mothers and prayer before the icon, the tears of the Virgin Mary, the prayer of the faithful with fire pots OFF, Virgin with veil, the boys from the other side call parents on the island famous, anticipation, despair parents, night descended, in their hearts, the dark depths of pushing body , bowel ocean, view of the icon, but there was nobody there, empty frame in a full church, dark hearts of unbelievers, break, crush the grace of the faithful, the mother pulls out the body from the depths of bright, hug their parents, the boys together, all three of them as they used to , at the altar, praying before the icon glossy, icon of the Virgin, without the veil, with a shell in his hands, white fabric in the sea, the light of the open sky, shining cloth, from the depths of bright, icon of the Virgin.

Angels protect America

Black birds

tearing his body

heart almost stopped

but the prayers of the saints

protect the city

that never sleeps

under the debris sprouting new fruits.

TAKEN FROM THE WATER

Papyrus reed, the women worked silently in the dark, the soldiers were coming from afar, waiting for the stones, leaving the snake winding trail of broken ground, hot coals in his mouth as evidence of a small barge with a reed boat on the river, weeping mother and a sign from heaven, stones were hiding the sun, snakes grew closer, the soldiers heard a child crying, they searched the whole area, but a small barge with a secret wing.

Ring in all rubies is not broke faith in him, and the embers kept in the mouth, to the dismay of many, commands were disseminated in the wilderness, but the snake had a tail made of wood, a small barge is overdue in the hands of a ruling that gave the child in care.

Selected was saved, the sun is bacalao kingdom, but soldiers are still looking for any child when they came to be, not where you have more, but they still heard the child crying, the board hit the ground, raised a huge cloud of dust, which obliterating the month, there were no lights in the desert, except in the room selected.

He put out his hand toward his mother, separated by the sea, crying is silent when it came to their mother's arms, the army was defeated, huge waves had covered their tijela. Voda is continuously radiated from the rocks, commands the sacred mountain, the wind grew stronger , the sea is once again separated, the snake was already almost all the wood, the more she could not move, the stone statue at the bottom of the ocean, women make a small boat of reeds, wooden stick into a snake was lifted at the top of the mountain sacred to and relied spoken commands.

A stone statue on the sea floor, but nobody tells you is not heard, the frescoes in the churches have changed color, the arrangement is no longer the same, the statue will start moving towards them, the stone on the holy mountain, a sign in the desert, a small barge is not overturned, the wind carries away from the soldiers, crying child, to light the statue as a halo shining, the sea is separated, the water emerges from the rock.

A mother embraces her child who does not cease to cry for them along the river comes a small boat, rescue is near, trembling reed, his mother's hand caressing a baby's head, a barge with them and sign it.

The wind is stronger, the cold is great, the mother embraces her child, approaching the boat, bush burning in it, warming their faces, arms to the bush baby, eternal

character, embrace of mother and child.

121

Black hole

The horrible

screams

in the dark

depths

times

missing

in the ashes

stars

on fire.

Apocalypse III

Bloody

tears

saints

in prayer

pledges

ancestors

the ashes

countries

burned

passions

sinners

at dawn

Judgment

days.

Then when the Sun died

Saturn cried for days

was in love with the Moon

a servant of the Sun

he met a blind Jupiter

Mars was already ready

 in a red mantle,

 winner of many duels

Judges Neptune and Uranus

 are standing next to weapons

Saturn is still crying

Earth watched sadly

behind the mask of the Sun

stands by his servant Moon

Mars was already dead

Sun was just around the corner

 with a gun darkness covered

It was only dust and ashes

Then the Sun put a black veil

 on itself

 and absolute silence reigned.

Moon

A ghostly silence
traces of the past
flag of freedom
on the dark side
of Moon
in the darkness

of time.

Poet in the Night

His tears

hid it verses

about flowers

that the ground is covered

dark clouds

to cry

the poet

Lost in the night.

Fall

The white earth

covered with feathers

the last flight

fallen angels.

__Apocalypse II__

While faith
wandered by road
missing memories
the church was
in prayer
for saving the world
which disappears
in flames.

Visions of Immortality

In the dark valley, the tears of the faithful, on the bloody rock on the night of the resurrection, the Son of God, prayers on the eternal fire.

The blue dome, the Sistine in the Bay of Saints in the moonlight in the fog of remembrance, the bells of Christians on the Day of Judgment.

Memories of the apostles in the night of weeping, River of verses in the holy books on the altar of the Homeland.

Bloody tears, prayers of saints in the dark chambers of death, shadows of ancestors on the shores of the hope of salvation.

In the immortal fire, burned memories of fear, eerie cries in the night, the cry of despair in the light of salvation.

Visions of light in immortal prayers, the bells of the church of the sea in the bay on the cliff of the Our Lady.

On the hill of the crucifixion, in the shadow of the cross, on Golgota, the bloody tears of the soldiers in silent penance.

The suffering of Christians, the history of remembrance in the mist .

*The consolation of prayer, the tears in Our Lady's eyes,
doomsday, in prayer at the bottom of the ocean.*

*The light of chandeliers, the storm of unbelief, the horrors
of dead souls in the shadows of transience.*

*The burnt hope of salvation in the truth of the fire, the
immortal spark in the eyes of the Madonna.*

*The shadow of the fire, on the wall of the church the sea in
the bay of remembrance, at the end of the shore, the
prayers of penance.*

*A lone star, at the bottom of the ocean, a weeping rock,
icons of salvation, bays of the immortals.*

*Churches in the mirror of the sea, a mirror of light in the
sea of memories, churches of the past, chandeliers of light.*

*The rosary of salvation, in the hands of the faithful on the
day of penance on the other side of the shore.*

**Milenko Županović was born in 1978 in Kotor (Montenegro).
By profession he is a graduate marine engineer, but in his
free time, he writes poetry and short stories. His poems and
other work have been published in *The Stray Branch, Mad
Swirl, The Horror Zine, Antarctica journal,,Mobius,Vox
Poetica,Ascent, Aspirations Magazine,,Rio Negro
Magazine,,Axxon,Balkanski književni glasnik,Versewrights
journal, Ariel Chart,Nova Fantasia,TreeHouse Arts,Emitor,
Every Day Poems, La Ira de Morfeo,Down in the Dirt,Edizioni
Scudo,Tragovi,Full of Crow,Poets***

**In 2010 he wrote and published his first book, a collection of
stories, and he also written and published few collections of
poems (ebooks). In 2015 he wrote and published his second
book, a collection of stories and poetry. In 2016 he wrote his
third book, a mini collection of poetry *Testament of
Ancestors* (published in USA, *project Poems for all)*. His
books *Martiri , Simboli Segreti , Rituali Sacri and Collina di
teschi* were published in italian language by *Edizioni Scudo*.
His chapbook *The Blood of Poets* was published by *Scars
Publications*.His brochure –collection of prose and devotional
poems *Dreams of Gods* was published by Mount Abraxas
Press.**

www.ingramcontent.com/pod-product-compliance
Lightning Source LLC
Chambersburg PA
CBHW071910120726
48001CB00005B/1693